WATFORD
A Pictorial History

In Watford by E. McKnight Kauffer (London Transport Museum, 1915).

WATFORD
A Pictorial History

Dennis F. Edwards

Phillimore

1992

Published by
PHILLIMORE & CO. LTD.,
Shopwyke Hall, Chichester, Sussex

ISBN 0 85033 834 4

Printed and bound in Great Britain by
BIDDLES LTD.,
Guildford, Surrey

To my Watford friends, David and Angela,
Alan and Olive

List of Illustrations

Frontispiece: In Watford by E. McKnight Kauffer, 1915

Illustration Acknowledgements

Illustrations 3-12, 32, 58-60, 72, 73, 89, 114, 120, 131, 135, 174-76 from the Watford Museum Collection (Watford Borough Council). All other illustrations are from the author's own collection.

Introduction

'The town is very long, having but one street. A genteel market town' – Daniel Defoe.

There is one thing that early historians and visitors to Watford were agreed upon: it was a town with one very long street. Today, writers have difficulty in placing Watford. Is it part of outer Greater London? Is it the largest town in Hertfordshire? Is it the gateway to the Midlands and a town of the provinces?

Watford is all of these things. It is a frontier, a place on the border. 'North of Watford' is a derisory term implying that civilisation ends here. But Watford has an identity. It perhaps stands aloof from rural Hertfordshire and from the Hertfordshire of soulless new towns. Yet it does not embrace London, despite appearing at the end of the London Underground map.

Watford has constantly been renewing itself since the Second World War. At present it is halfway through a great reconstruction of its commercial heart. Through the medium of illustrations we can see how the town grew from 'one long street' at the dawn of the Industrial Age to the vast town it is today.

'Watford' – what's in the name? Certainly there are no Roman remains here, but we may be certain that it was a Saxon settlement, a crossing of the marshy River Colne. Wat's ford or was it just damp wet ford? Speculation on so many of our English place names is inconclusive. What we do know is that Watford grew up by the Colne at what is now Bushey Arches.

If a place was not mentioned in Domesday Book, it does not necessarily mean that it did not exist. Watford was not mentioned, but Cassiobury was: 'The abbey of St Albans holds Caissou. It answers for 20 hides: of these the abbot holds 19. There is land for 22 ploughs'. Pasture for cattle and pannage for 1,000 hogs are also mentioned.

Cassiobury dominated Watford for many centuries. Would there have been a town without the estate? Probably, because Watford lay along the main road to the Midlands, carrying processions of drovers with their herds and merchants and travellers of all kinds, especially those who had business at the castle at Berkhampstead, where Chaucer lived for a time. A settlement for local farmers and a market for the local villages was certainly here by the 12th century, grouped round a Norman church. It was sufficiently important for Edward III to grant a market charter in 1335 (confirmed by Edward IV in 1469). The market was to be held on Tuesdays for corn, straw plait and cattle, including hogs. Two annual fairs were also to be held: one for three days after the Monday following Trinity Sunday and the other on 29 August. These fairs lasted until 1878. The Tuesday market (and later Saturday market) survived in the centre of the town until 1928. There is still a market, now comfortably under cover.

The earliest description of Watford comes from William Camden's famous *Britannia* of 1583. This is what he said:

WATFORDE or WATELINEFORDE for that the Wattelinestreete crosseth the Colne nere this place and so coasteth to old Verlame [St Albans] as is sayd before [John Norden, *Hartfordshire*, 1598]. Somewhat lower I saw Watford and Rickmansworth two mercate townes; concerning which I have read nothing of greater antiquity than this, that king Offa liberally gave them unto St Albans; as also

Caisobery next unto Watford. In which place Sir Richard Morisin knight, a great learned man, and who had beene used in Embassages to the mightiest princes, under king Henrie the Eighth and king Edward the Sixth began to build a house, which Sir Charles his sonne finally finished.

The house mentioned is the first Cassiobury House. Henry VIII had granted Sir Richard Morrison the estate in 1546, and from then onwards the Morrisons were dominant in the history of Watford. Sir Richard built 'A fair large house' on rising ground above the River Gade to the west of the town. His mansion was completed by his son. It probably resembled other houses of the time in the area – Chenies Manor, for example. According to a visitor in 1599 it was quite large, with 56 rooms and a long gallery. The estate lands were much more extensive than they are today, reaching northwards to the area we now know as North Watford, and south to the lands around Moor Park.

Watford saw Parliamentary troops marching several times on the way to the Midlands and the North in the Civil War, but the town was little affected during this period. After the Civil War, Sir Charles Morrison's daughter Elizabeth (baptised at Watford parish church in 1610) inherited the Cassiobury estate, and she married Arthur Capel in 1627. The Capel family was settled at Hadham, but after the marriage it was closely associated with Cassiobury. As the 1st Earl of Essex, Arthur Capel decided to rebuild Cassiobury and commissioned Hugh May who was working for Charles II. It is amusing to find that large building works even then were subject to delay and unexpected expense. The earl wrote to his brother from Ireland that he should hasten the work at 'Cashioberry and of the covering of it and that it should be done with all dispatch imaginable ... for unless this part of the house be roofed and tiled before I come, I do not know how I shall be able to lie one night there'. By 9 June 1677 there was still work to be completed. The new house was laid out with an 'H' ground plan, popular during that period, and was filled with all kinds of fine things. The magnificent staircase was carved by Grinling Gibbons and this set the tone for the furnishing of the building. The Capels were patrons of the arts and on 16 April 1680 John Evelyn accompanied Grinling Gibbons to Cassiobury:

On the earnest invitation of the Earl of Essex, I went with him to his house at Cassioberie in Hertford-shire. The house is new, a plaine fabric built by my friend Mr. Hugh May, there are divers faire and good rooms and excellent carvings by Grinling Gibbons, especially the chimney piece of ye library.

But Evelyn soon found that the estate was not to his liking:

The soil is stony, churlish and uneven, nor is the water [the Gade] near enough to the house though a very swift and clear stream runs within a flight shot from it. The valley which may fitly be called Colnbrook, it being indeed excessive cold, yet producing fair trouts ... it is a pity that the house was not situated to more advantage, but it seems it was built just where the old one was.

Eventually the earl was implicated in the Rye House plot, and was sent to the Tower in 1683, committing suicide there.

A century later the 5th Earl of Essex was finding the old rambling house difficult to maintain. Fashions were also changing and he commissioned a popular architect of the day, James Wyatt, to remodel it – in effect, to build a new house. Wyatt specialised in the Romantic 'Gothick' style, criticised as recently as 1957 by the writer James Parker as 'a mutation of real Gothic style'. Wyatt worked hard on his plans, and the new style Cassiobury was virtually completed by 1804. The celebrated Humphry Repton was commissioned to landscape the parklands. It was Wyatt's nephew, Sir Jeffrey Wyattville, who carried out the designs for the delightful lodges and cottages that once could be found in the grounds. Only one now survives – Cassiobury Lodge (Gade Avenue), 'the most elaborate in execution – its whole exterior being covered or cased with sticks of various sizes split in two', wrote a Victorian visitor.

Another visitor in 1816 was Frances Calvery. In her book, *An Irish Beauty of the Regency*, she wrote: 'On Wednesday we went to Cashiobury, the seat of the Earl of Essex, which is a very pretty house and more full of comforts, curiosities and pretty things than any other house I ever saw. Lord and Lady Holland, Lord Auckland and several more now in the house'. On Thursday she records: 'Lady Essex took us all over her flower gardens, which I declare, are the most complete in England'. Certainly, the flower gardens were one of the glories of the estate for many years.

The parties and entertainments continued at Cassiobury until the early years of the 20th century, and notable people, such as the young Winston Churchill and King Edward VII, were visitors.

The new Wyatt house comprised a vast number of rooms, but the main ones were the Winter Drawing Room, with family portraits by Lely and Van Dyck; the Crimson Drawing Room, with Canaletto, Gainsborough, Morland and Reynolds; the Inner Library which also had portraits by Reynolds; and the Great Library, in which were busts of the Duke of Bedford, the Duke of Wellington, Napoleon and Charles I. The furniture of the Best Drawing Room was said to be 'of the latest fashion and displays superior taste'. Another spectacular room was the State Bedroom, with blue and white furnishings, a Gobelin tapestry, *The Village Feast*, and a ceiling in blue and gilt.

In 1841, a fire destroyed the orangery, which was filled with newly collected exotic plants and fine orange trees. Some of the trees had been presented to the 6th Earl by Louis XVII. These were the days when herds of deer roamed the Cassiobury parklands, and parties were a regular feature at weekends in the great house. The public were allowed to ride and walk through the grounds, but had to apply for a ticket in advance. As in the case of so many estates, however, financial difficulties were beginning to be a problem even before the First World War. The last great social occasion at the house seems to have been in 1913, and already the family had begun to live in London, letting the house.

After 1907 there were sales of land for housing purposes as modern Watford was already pressing along the edges of the great park. The First World War finally sealed the fate of Cassiobury, and the mansion and grounds were put up for sale on Thursday, 8 June 1922: 'The historical family mansion ... embracing in all an area of about 870 acres by direction of Adele, Countess Dowager of Essex'.

There were many attempts to save the mansion, and George V and Queen Mary showed interest, but these were not times of conservation. Watford Borough had already bought part of the parklands in December 1912 and Cassiobury Estates Limited sold the council a further 33 acres to add to the 90 acres they already owned in 1923. Further land was secured for the town in 1930, 1932 (the golf course) and 1935 (Whippendell Woods). The contents of the house were disposed of far and wide and the famous Grinling Gibbons staircase went to the Metropolitan Museum of Fine Art in New York.

By 1927 it was apparent that no buyer could be found for Wyatt's great house and it was offered for demolition. Posters proclaimed: 'To lovers of the antique, architects, builders, etc. 300 tons of old oak: 100 very fine old oak beams and 10,000 Tudor period bricks'. Today almost nothing survives of the buildings of old Cassiobury except the stable block in Temple Close, where it is said that the Tudor cellars lie under the modern development.

The 1920s and '30s saw the countryside around many towns used for the development of modern houses. It makes strange reading to look in a guide-book to Watford of 1930 and read:

Cassiobury Park, which for so long prevented the expansion of Watford on the north west side, is now its chief encouragement to residential expansion. For the great mansion and the park of the Earls of Essex have succumbed to the irresistible pressure of the time and fringes of the park have been converted to building sites.

The Metropolitan Railway built a branch line to Watford and opened the station in 1925 on the edge of the park. They proudly announced: 'Thanks to local enterprise, backed by a great railway company, a large population ... is enabled to live amid beautiful and healthful surroundings. On every side at Watford have arisen wide, handsome roads, with the latest appliances of light ... and all have free access to the park'.

With regard to Watford itself, Daniel Defoe's 'small genteel town' and its one long street had grown rapidly since the coming of the railway. During the early centuries of Cassiobury's existence, communications were poor, but the coaching roads, including the Hatfield and Reading turnpike, helped to improve things. Coaches called at Watford on the way to and from Aylesbury, Birmingham and so on. Inns such as *The George*, the *Essex Arms* and the *Rose and Crown* grew in importance and there were even local coach services – such as the Tring to London via Watford, through which it was possible, by rising very early in the morning, to be back in Watford by supper time.

The opening of the Grand Junction canal in 1793 did not really affect Watford. Its route passed between the estates of The Grove, owned by Lord Clarendon, and Cassiobury, although Lady Capel's wharf was established to handle goods for Watford. The Grove had been the home of the Heydon family in Elizabethan times. In 1756 the estate was owned by Sir Robert Taylor and the house was enlarged and the grounds landscaped in both 1780 and 1850. The building is now a business college.

In most towns, the parish church is the hub of history. St Mary's, the parish church of Watford, dates back to Norman times, although there is nothing of that period to be seen today. The earliest parts of the church are 13th-century; the nave and tower mainly 15th-century, the latter being capped by a typical 'Hertfordshire spike'. The north chapel of 1595 commemorates the Capel family, although it was founded by Lady Bridget Morrison, and her husband Sir Richard has a fine monument there. The chancel contains brasses going back to the 15th century, but a reminder of more recent history is the east window, which dates from 1950, replacing one destroyed by bombs which fell in the churchyard during the Second World War. The south aisle of St Mary's was rebuilt in 1505 by William Heydon, and there is a memorial with an epitaph by Dr. Johnson to Jane Bell, who died in the 18th century. Boswell commented upon it 'as a fine eulogium from the outline of her character and Johnson's knowledge of her work'.

Education was established in Watford by the foundation of the Free School in the churchyard in 1704, by Dame Elizabeth Fuller who lived nearby at Watford Place. The present day Watford Place dates from 1790/1. When she became a widow she decided to devote her life to charitable work, and her school was 'for the teaching of 40 poor boys and 14 poor girls of Watford in good literature and manners'. Her family name was Chilcott, and the arms are still visible on the building. Pupils had to attend the school every day of the week from 6 a.m. (7 a.m. in winter) until 4 p.m.

Near the school are the Bedford almshouses of 1580. Their founder was Francis Russell, 2nd Earl of Bedford, and his wife, and were 'for eight poor women to be chosen from Watford, and from Langley and Chenies in Buckinghamshire'. The old buildings were saved from demolition in the 1930s and have been restored several times.

The tranquil parklands and the new canal which John Hassell describes in 1819 as 'full of nightingales and embellished with noble timber' remain, but the Victorian period saw the transformation of Watford from a single street market town to a large manufacturing and residential centre. One of the earliest industries to employ a number of people was Rookery Mill, a silk mill opened in 1819 beside the then new Grand Junction Canal. In 1792, 500 were employed here and by Hassell's day, in 1819, the establishment was 'conducted on very superior principles'. The mill has long gone, but Rookery Road keeps the name and Watford football ground nearby has a Rookery End.

It was the building of the London and Birmingham Railway and the opening of the first station at Watford (on the 'tunnel' side of St Albans bridge) on 26 July 1837 that proved to be one of the most important events in the town's history. It was said that more men were employed to build the line than on any other project since the construction of the Great Pyramid. The architect was John Rennie and the engineer George Stephenson. Stephenson sought to provide as level a route as possible and would have passed south of Watford, but both Clarendon and Essex were opposed to the scheme and did not want the steam, the noise and the common people to pass through their estates. Thus the railway was constructed on a wide loop to the north of the town. Additional work had to be carried out to create the deep Bushey and Oxhey cutting and the tunnels under the Essex lands. Those well-known landmarks, the Bushey and Colne arches, carried the line over the marshy land at the bottom of the town. The arches, which rested on brushwood, doubled the original estimated cost per mile of £50. The making of Watford tunnel cost 11 lives and many navvies were injured.

At first trains ran as far as Tring, then to Bletchley from April 1838, and finally right through to Birmingham on 17 September 1838. In 1846 The London and North Western Railway was formed, and took over the line. Watford became a junction when the branch to St Albans opened on 5 May 1858, with a further line to Rickmansworth promoted by Lord Ebury of Moor Park. This opened on 1 October 1862 as part of a plan to link Watford with Uxbridge. A station was opened at High Street Watford, later to be rebuilt for the electric lines from Euston.

The population of Watford began to grow, from 6,546 in 1851 to 7,461 10 years later. By 1881 it was 10,076 and in 1901 it was 19,327. The good connections by rail with London attracted printing and engineering industries and workers, as well as a group of travellers we would now call 'commuters'. The St Albans Road area was developed as were Nascot Wood-Langley Road, and also the land between the Junction and the old town. Clarendon Road was a fine new highway lined with large suburban villas dating from 1864. It was built over the grounds of Watford House, which had been built in 1775 by Thomas Clutterbuck and was finally demolished in 1896. Another member of the family was Robert Clutterbuck, author of the classic book on the history of Hertfordshire, *The History and Antiquities of the County of Hartford*, published between 1815 and 1827. He is buried in the churchyard of St Mary's. The last owner of Watford House from 1880 to 1896 was Dr. Alfred Butt, who was a medical officer of health for the Watford Urban District Council (which replaced the old Local Board in 1894 and was itself superseded by the Borough of Watford in 1922). The developer of Clarendon Road and much of the area around it was Thomas Estcourt, whose name is recalled by one of the roads.

As Watford grew, new churches were established, the finest of these perhaps being Holy Rood, Market Street, built in 1857. More new roads were laid out in the middle years of the Victorian period, including King Street (on the route of the drive to Watford

Place), Queen's Road and Market Street. The old turnpike disappeared from the end of the High Street on 1 July 1872. Education was improved too, with the formation of Watford School Board in 1885. It became responsible for the British schools in Beechen Grove and Lion Yard. New buildings were erected such as Watford Fields school, but the church schools and Dame Fuller's school were not included. The latter moved as 'Watford endowed schools' to new premises in Derby Road in 1884 and the present Watford Grammar schools are descended from this establishment.

As with most old towns, there were problems with the water and sewerage systems. A report of 1849 tells how water was supplied from wells and ponds by means of buckets and was very hard. It was recommended that supplies should be brought into the town from Oxhey. In 1885 the Pump House was at Watford Fields and supplied much of the town's water until 1916. It is now the Pump House Theatre.

Industry continued to grow as a consequence of the railway and the L.N.W.R. laid out large freight sidings to serve the local factories. Milling, brewing and food processing were important industries, as was engineering. Printing became established as a major industry because the Colne valley had been a centre for papermaking since at least the 18th century. By 1930 Watford was called 'the printing capital of the world'. Companies included Waterlow in Milton Street and The Sun Engraving Company (formed by Menpes Printing and Engineering Co. in 1918, when they merged with the Anglo Engraving Co.). In 1938 Odhams arrived, situated in a magnificent new building. Odhams dominated Watford until its closure in 1983, a few years after Robert Maxwell equipped the company with some of the world's most advanced technology. Odhams then merged with The Sun to become Odhams-Sun.

The new century got off to a rather bad start for Watford town centre. King Edward's coronation celebrations had to be postponed because he was taken ill, but certain rowdy elements felt deprived and riots broke out on Thursday 27 June 1902. Windows were broken and '56 persons of the lowest characters of the town were arrested'.

The market-place had changed by the beginning of the 20th century and the old Market Hall had been destroyed by fire in 1853. The town pump and stocks had been swept away. The Tuesday market continued to thrive, although the pigs had been moved to a site off Market Street. More and more shops and department stores, such as Clements, Cawdell's and Trewin Brothers appeared. The L.N.W.R. obtained an Act of Parliament in 1911 for a pair of additional tracks from London to Watford, making a total of six. The so-called New Lines were for steam-hauled suburban trains and a loop line was constructed from Bushey, crossing the Colne and running by Watford Fields, to link with the Rickmansworth line. Watford High Street was rebuilt as a two-line island platform and the railway doubled. There were plans for electrification and already there was a market along the route for suburban home seekers. *The Homefinder* magazine reported that 'The new services are drawing new residents out from Euston to the pleasant fields still to be occupied in the 17 miles from Euston to Watford'. In the event, it was the tube trains of the Bakerloo line that were the first to use the electrified tracks of the New Lines, reaching Junction station on 16 April 1917, although they did not run on Sundays. The L.N.W.R. electric trains from Broad Street and Euston did not begin until 18 July 1922 because of the First World War.

As street after street of working-class and middle-class homes were built, there was a demand for entertainment. Theatre in Watford dates back to the 18th century when performances were held at the old *Wheatsheaf* by Bushey Arches. In 1907 the tea gardens at the back of the *Lime Tree Hotel* in Clarendon Road were purchased for the erection of what was to be called the New Theatre, although when the building opened on 14 December 1908 it was called The Palace. On the opening night the Palace Orchestra played popular airs as patrons were conducted to their seats. The theatre became known as a 'twice nightly house' and music hall stars, such as Dan Leno and Marie Lloyd, appeared there.

Watford was a popular place for cinemas, and as early as 1910 there were displays of animated pictures at the Corn Exchange and the Agricultural Hall. One of the first purpose-built cinemas was in Lower High Street from 1911, where tea was served to patrons. When the Central Hall Picture House opened in 1928 in King Street, the cinema was firmly part of entertainment in the town – 'Always a reliable programme at the Central Hall accompanied by a first class orchestra', according to a newspaper report.

The 1930s were, of course, the golden age of the cinema. Watford people could forget the long term unemployed of the north of England whose organised 'Hunger Marches' passed through the town on their way to London, and settle in the luxurious seats at new cinemas, such as the Carlton, which replaced a roller skating rink next to the Palace Theatre. The high point of cinema ambience came with the opening of the Gaumont by the mayor, assisted by comedian Will Hay, in 1937. It had a comfortable lounge where refreshments were served and was known as 'Watford's popular rendezvous'. A far cry from the days when Watford seemed to have had more pubs and beer houses than shops.

Cassiobury Park Estate housing developments began in 1907 along Rickmansworth Road, Cassiobury Park Avenue and Shepherds Avenue. At this time the popular styles were set by Charles Voysey and Norman Shaw, and many of the houses built at Cassiobury reflected their ideas. The architect W. Wallis Baldwin designed many of the houses, which had generous gardens, but in the original development there were strict stipulations on the price of the houses, and only tiled roofs were allowed.

The area of Callowlands had been developed in the late 19th century (the name dates from the 14th century and means 'bare lands') and industry grew along the St Albans branch railway. Callowland Halt was opened by Bushey Mill Lane for the convenience of workers on the growing industrial estates. One factory was called Delectaland, the home of Dr. Tibbet's Vi-Cocoa, 'the food Beverage of the people ... made in Watford'. Later the factory was destroyed by fire. The name Callowlands was superseded by North Watford in the 1920s.

The Watford bypass was constructed in the late 1920s and along it smart 'road houses' were opened for those who had money to spend and a sports car to race. There were other landmarks too, notably the Odhams Press building by Sir Owen Williams, built 1938-9, to a design based on Stockholm Town Hall. The Watford building is now a supermarket.

Another important building in the town centre was the Town Hall by C. Cowles-Voysey, dating from 1938. Watford had become a borough on 18 October 1922, but the council offices for many years had been at Upton House in the High Street. Sir Thomas Beecham called the main hall in the new building one of the finest venues for recording music outside London.

The most important transport landmark after the First World War was the opening of the Metropolitan railway to Watford in 1925. Planned in 1912, there had been dreams of crossing Cassiobury Park and Hempstead Road and going on to Garston, but in 1922 work began on a revised route, with a station at Croxley and a terminus at Cassiobury Park Avenue. The contractors, Logan and Hemingway, found the work much more difficult than had originally been thought. Deep cuttings had to be made south of Croxley, not far from where the new line left the Metropolitan mainline between Moor Park and

Rickmansworth, and high bridges had to be constructed over the Gade and the canal, with a very high embankment towards the terminus. There had been plans for a second intermediate station to serve the West Hertfordshire golf club, but this was not built. The original opening date had been set for August 1924 but, because of the wet weather and difficulties encountered, even the postponed date in April 1925 was missed, and it was October before the line was finally ready for inspection. A special test train consisting of two heavy Metropolitan 'K'-class steam engines was run along the line. There was great enthusiasm for the arrival of the new line; Watford would at last become part of Metroland, with rows of smart villas occupied by well paid City clerks, and also have a train service so frequent (or so it was claimed) that you did not need a timetable! The *Watford Observer* stated optimistically: 'The Metropolitan railway is likely to have a much greater effect on the development of the town than is at present realised. Just as trade follows the flag, so does the population follow the railway ... the Cassiobury estate will be speedily built up'. Extensive freight yards, cattle docks and a warehouse were laid out, but the railway was forced to construct a lengthy section of road called Station Approach so that its five delivery lorries and those of customers would not have to pass the suburban houses of Shepherds Avenue and Cassiobury Park Avenue. When the new line was officially opened on 31 October 1925, and opened to passengers on 2 November, there were high hopes for good returns on both goods and passenger receipts, but the new station suffered from being too far from the town centre.

From 2 November 1927 the Metropolitan operated a bus service which connected with every train. There was a fare of 2d. and the buses ran via Cassiobury Park Avenue, Rickmansworth Road, Cassio Road, Merton Road, St Mary's Road, Church Street, Vicarage Road, Hagden Lane, Queen's Avenue and Station Approach. There was also a two-car shuttle train linking Watford direct to Rickmansworth via the north curve line south of Croxley, although this regular service was withdrawn in 1934.

In 1927, the Metropolitan looked into the possibility of extending the line into the heart of Watford. The directors purchased the empty premises of the Empress Restaurant at 44 High Street and bought land behind. They felt that extra revenue could also be obtained if sidings were laid to the adjacent cattle market, but the possibility of having to build deep cuttings, or even a tunnel, made the scheme too expensive and the property was later sold.

The 1930s saw Watford developing into a great business and shopping centre, attracting people from all over south Hertfordshire. Increasing numbers of cars and buses began to fill the streets. The Queen Victoria Jubilee Oak and the A.A. man who directed traffic at the Rickmansworth Road/High Street crossroads were replaced by a traffic roundabout. Old landmarks, like the *Essex Hotel* and Corn Exchange were swept away, the old established stores were rebuilt in more palatial premises and shops of nationally known retailers opened. New streets of semi-detached houses spread northwards, whilst the rapid development of Harrow, to the south, threatened to join London's suburbia to Watford.

In the Second World War, Watford was in the front line. Almost before the paint which obliterated the station name boards was dry, bombs fell in the town centre, damaging the church and burning a decorator's shop and the toy department of Trewin's in Queen's Road, whilst in December 1940 people were killed in St John's Road. One of the worst incidents took place later in the war, when on Sunday 31 July 1944 a V1 rocket bomb fell on Sandringham Road. Forty residents were killed.

Since 1945 Watford has been fighting a battle against ever-increasing traffic. The photographs depicting the High Street in the immediate post-war period show how it was still possible to park by the shops, but by the 1960s drastic remedies had to be taken. The roundabout at the north-west end of High Street by the Town Hall was replaced by an underpass and there later came the ugly Exchange Road flyover crossing the High Street by The Parade. Watford increasingly began to fall into decay and disappear. Upton House and the old fire station in High Street were replaced by Gade House with the Co-operative store and by the end of the 1960s all the houses there had gone. In Queen's Road, Trewin's store was rebuilt (as part of the John Lewis partnership), the Methodist church with its tall steeple was demolished and Loates Lane was widened. The huge, menacing concrete bulk of Charter Place shopping centre was erected in 1974, the High Street approach replacing Cawdell's arcade and store and the old covered market.

By the 1970s Watford had become one of the most prosperous towns in the country. The Euston main line was electrified and plans were made for rebuilding Watford Junction station (finally completed in 1989). Leavesden Airport was developed for executive private jets and Watford even had its own evening paper, *The Echo*.

A second period of great change is now in progress. The first stage of the vast Harlequin shopping centre opened in 1990, covering the site of many early Victorian streets and transforming the southern half of Queen's Road into part of the precinct. Work is now going ahead on the second phase of the centre and also on a link road from Berrygrove roundabout (near junction 5 on the M1) to the town centre by Bushey Mill Lane, Colonial and Imperial Way, and south under the railway to Water Lane, with a branch going down to the bottom of Lower High Street and the Five Arches. So much of old Watford is now disappearing. Yet there are paradoxes: neat streets of Victorian terraced houses still remain, with traditional 'open all hours' corner shops, and a horse drawn van from which residents can buy fruit and vegetables in their street. Joseph Benskin's old house has become the museum and Watford football team still continues to flourish.

Perhaps Watford of the coming century will have few links with the past; it will be too absorbed in business and retailing. But any town that has no visible history is a town without a soul, and Watford could be in danger of losing its Hertfordshire identity and becoming just a large conurbation in an even larger Greater London.

The following collection of illustrations does not claim to be comprehensive. It is based on the author's collection of old postcards, together with drawings and photographs from other sources. It is a pictorial tour of Watford's past for those who are newcomers to the town, or for people who have not previously reflected on their town's past. It is hoped that these windows into history will stimulate further interest in and create a greater appreciation of Watford, so that a stronger voice may be raised in the future to prevent any more loss of the town's landmarks and links with the past.

This delightful description of Watford just before the railway age was written by Eustace Condor, whose father lived at Watford Field House from 1824 to 1839:

'As the town lay several miles off the Great North Road, there was no great amount of traffic passing through. Two or three London coaches on their way to Chesham, Hampstead or some other town further down in the country, were the modest substitute for long railway trains, with their two or three hundred passengers. A few lumbering carriers' vans representing the 'goods trains' of later and more impatient times. Every night, the mail coach, with its flaring eyes and red-coated guard, made the quiet streets echo with its horn, picked up, perhaps, its one passenger, and excited mysterious feelings of respect and wonder in the minds of little boys. All round the dear, dull, quiet little town lay the still more quiet country. Two minutes would bring you into it; on the one side across the little river Colne, into green low-lying meadows, which the artificially raised banks do not keep the stream from overflowing for miles after heavy rains; on the other, through the lime-shaded churchyard, out among cornfields and homesteads, and shady lanes; or over stiles and through footpaths, to where the deer browse amongst the spreading limes and beeches, or hide in the thickets of tall fern, in Cassiobury Park.'

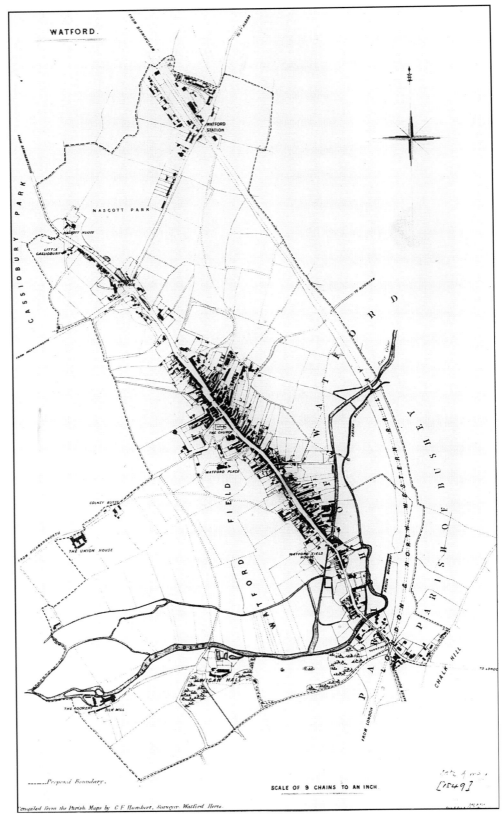

1. Map of Watford, 1849

2. This is a typical Edwardian multi-view postcard showing some of the landmarks of the town. High Street near the junction with Queen's Road and King Street is at the top. The central view is of the old Swiss Cottage in the grounds of Cassiobury near the River Gade. The building is commemorated today in Swiss Avenue. The lower picture shows Queen's Road with the spire of the old Wesleyan church.

3. This general view of Watford in 1850 was drawn from the fields at Wiggen Hall, a house at one time owned by the Deacon and the King families. The drawing shows how the old lower High Street dropped down to the River Colne, and already there is an image of change: the train steaming along in the top right-hand corner.

4. Seventy years passed between the previous picture and this one from several hundred feet above the same spot. Wiggenhall Road runs across the picture. There are the grounds of old Watford Place and Shrodells hospital, St Mary's church tower, then the rows of working-class housing that spread over the fields in the 1880s and '90s. In the top left is the tower of the Roman Catholic church, Holy Rood (1857), one of the noblest examples of the refined, knowledgeable and sensitive Gothic revival of that time.

Air View of Watford.

No.

5. *Cassiobury Mansion: The West Front* by
J. M. W. Turner, 1804. Turner carried
out a number of commissions for the 5th
Earl of Essex and the Turner Bequest
includes a collection of 11 drawings of
Cassiobury, the majority dating from
*c.*1804. Several of Turner's works hung in
the house.

6.   This is what the estate at Cassiobury
looked like in 1707. It shows the H-plan
of the house erected in 1674-80 by the
1st Earl of Essex.

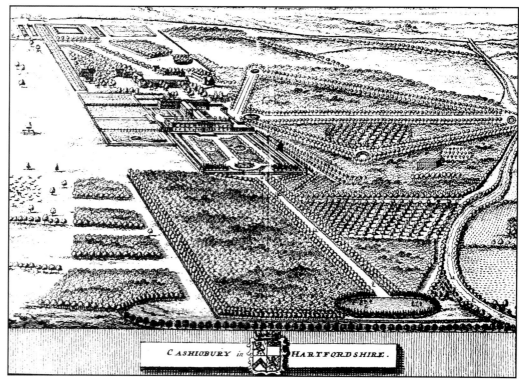

CASHIOBURY in HARTFORDSHIRE.

7. The house in 1707. Hugh May incorporated parts of the Tudor mansion. Whilst in Ireland, Essex wrote to his brother, Sir Henry Capel, promising to send £100-200 to 'raise and cover the building ... which is begun at Cassiobury'. The pediment seen here incorporated a frieze, showing the goddess Diana hunting.

8. The 5th Earl of Essex commissioned James Wyatt to rebuild Cassiobury. Wyatt was a popular architect of the late 18th century, when the early Gothic revival was just beginning. It was this style he employed, no doubt inspired by Fonthill in Wiltshire. The house is shown here as it appeared in 1837.

9. A fine view of the Gothic splendours of lost Cassiobury in 1830. A visitor to Cassiobury a decade before wrote of the house: 'It is a long pile in imitation of Gothic architecture with a number of pointed turrets and deep window frames in which are double compartments painted with the scriptural subjects of the Twelve Apostles'.

10. In Edwardian days there was still much entertainment at Cassiobury when the Essex family were at home and Winston Churchill and King Edward VII paid visits. The house was let in 1900 for a time and advertised as having 'shooting and trout fishing. Thoroughly up to date with seven bathrooms, central heating, electric light and telephone'.

11. The 7th Earl of Essex (George Devereux de Vere) and Lady Essex (Adèle Grant) at Cassiobury Park. Adèle came from a wealthy American family and was the Earl's second wife. Their marriage took place in 1893, the year after the Earl succeeded to the title. He was Vice-Lieutenant of Hertfordshire and also Aide de Camp to Edward VII. The marriage day was one of great celebration in Watford, and there was a triumphal arch over the street outside the *Essex Arms Hotel*.

12. The last days of the great house, depicted in a painting by Kate Cowderoy of the octagonal kitchen in 1920. Even as late as 1950 there were still critics of the early Gothic: 'a mutation of neo-Gothic architecture' is what one architect said of the by then vanished house.

13. Cassiobury House and the parklands seen from the River Gade in Edwardian days. The pathway still exists, but suburban houses now cover the background.

14. Swiss Cottage stood near the Gade not far from where, today, the Metropolitan railway crosses the river and the canal. The cottage had stained-glass windows depicting the customs and dress of Switzerland, as well as Swiss views.

15. This view of Swiss Cottage was posted from Watford on 5 July 1906. The cottage was always a popular spot to visit and early in the 19th century a guide book to Cassiobury stated that visitors to the park (by permission of the Earl of Essex) could picnic by the cottage or even rent a room if the weather turned wet.

16. A view of Swiss Cottage, *c.*1907. The daughters of the Earl lived in the cottage for some years. Swiss Avenue commemorates the building, which was destroyed by fire in the Second World War.

17. Keeper's Lodge, *c.*1837. The many lodges and rustic buildings about the park were the work of either Wyatt or his nephew, Sir Jeffrey Wyatville.

18. The Old Mill and waterfall, Cassiobury Park, 1856. Corn was originally ground here, but by the 19th century the mill was ornamental. It was demolished in 1956.

19. The Old Mill as it was in the mid-1930s.

20. Shepherd's Cottage, the home of the estate shepherd, was another much-loved lodge of old Cassiobury. It stood in Rickmansworth Road at the junction of Shepherd's Way until 1956.

21. The River Gade flowing towards the falls and the Swiss Cottage in the 1930s. The cottage was painted by Emma Oliver, the wife of John Sedgewick, who lived at The Limes by Watford Pond.

22.　The bridge over the Gade, Cassiobury Park, 1927.

23. 'The park is as great a luxury to Watford as the parks of Windsor are to the inhabitants of that town', said a guide book of 1937, when this view was taken. By that time the mansion had gone and the remaining open land had become a public park.

24. This 1908 photograph is looking towards the spot from where plate 13 was taken. The scene here has changed little.

25. One landmark of Cassiobury that many visitors to Watford saw as they entered the town was the gateway in Rickmansworth Road. The caption on this 1914 postcard reads: 'The park contains 500 acres, watered by the River Gade, and is adorned by fine fir-trees and numerous beeches; also cedars for which the estate is noted. In 1908 the Urban District Council purchased 50 acres at a cost of £16,500 for the purposes of a Public Park'. The gatehouse itself was described in 1819 as 'an octagonal, tasteful building – ivy and honeysuckle and roses cover its top and sides, its back embowered among lofty trees'.

26.   Another view of the gates, and on the left an almost unbelievably rural Rickmansworth Road. John Britton, in his *History and Description of Cassiobury Park* published in 1837, wrote about the gates: 'a pleasing feature in a finely wooded road'. By the time this view was taken, times were beginning to change and the Earl of Wilton, who rented the estate for a short time, crashed one of his sports cars into the estate fencing along the Rickmansworth Road.

27.   Our final picture of the gates shows them in wintry conditions in 1908. Rickmansworth Road was already being developed – note the boundary fence of one of the first villas. An advertisement offered 'Newly Constructed houses with a liberal area of garden land to each house. Only tiled roofs allowed. Houses in course of erection in The Shepherd's Road and Rickmansworth Road. From £600 to £800 ... delightfully situated about ten minutes from Watford Junction Station'.

28.   Grove Mill Lane looking towards Grove Mill in the early 1900s. Despite busy main roads nearby, this is still a pleasant country roadway.

29.   Grove Mill Lane looking north, with the walls along the boundary of The Grove. This view dates from the summer of 1905.

30. The woodlands at Grove Mill Lane were known as Deer Spring Wood, and young deer and game birds were raised here for both the Grove and Cassiobury estates. This picture was taken in 1906.

31. Grove Mill, 1911. The first record of the mill is in 1601. In 1677 James Davidson was miller, and a field opposite the mill was called Charlotte's Field, after a daughter of one of the Earls of Essex. A Victorian lady wrote of the mill in 1880: 'An ever-rolling mill stream ran all round the garden and the hedges of china roses, sweetbriar, honeysuckle and white hawthorn'.

32. Signs of change: a sales notice for the estate in 1922. Few of the contents remained in Watford, the Grinling Gibbons staircase (surviving from the earlier house) being sold to America. It is now in the Metropolitan Museum in New York.

By direction of the Right Honourable

ADELE, COUNTESS DOWAGER OF ESSEX.

HERTFORDSHIRE

Adjacent to the Town of Watford and about a mile from Watford Junct:
(L. & N.W.R.), 16 miles from London.

Particulars, Plans, Views and Conditions of Sale

OF THE

CASSIOBURY PARK ESTATE

INCLUDING

THE HISTORICAL FAMILY MANSION,

Little Cassiobury, and the West Herts Golf Links,

Embracing in all an Area of about

870 Acres.

For Sale by Auction,

At the Estate Sale Room, 20, Hanover Square, W.,
On THURSDAY, the 8th day of JUNE, 1922
At 2.30 o'clock (unless meanwhile Sold Privately), by

HUMBERT & FLINT

in conjunction with

KNIGHT, FRANK & RUTLEY

SOLICITORS	Messrs. ROOPER & WHATELY, 17, Lincoln's Inn Fields, W.C.2
AUCTIONEERS	Messrs. KNIGHT, FRANK & RUTLEY, 20, Hanover Square, W.1
	Messrs. HUMBERT & FLINT, 11, Serle Street, Lincoln's Inn, W.C. and Watford, Herts.

33. The opening of the Metropolitan railway to Watford created new 'Metroland'-style housing in the park. Labour-saving houses were in great demand as servants became difficult to find after the First World War.

34. A 1931 advertisement for Clark Brothers, a firm of builders which erected houses in Cassiobury. Fearnley Street was named after Edmund Fearnley, a 19th-century landowner in the old part of the town.

35. 'Be healthy and happy ...' – a builder's advertisement of 1929. Cassiobury Park was seen as a new extension to Metroland and there were houses for sale to suit all pockets. A new semi-detached house with a 'Watford Minor' iron boiler in the kitchen could cost £1,000, but some were as cheap as £600.

36. Cassiobury Park in 1922, at about the time of the sale of the house. What is now Cassiobury Park Drive can clearly be seen. Only the stable block of the old house now survives. Watford town is in the distance.

37. When Mr. Puddifoot announced his Excellent Freehold Residences, local rates were 60p in the £1.

38. St Mary's tower dates from the 15th century, but the embattled top was added during the restoration of the church in 1871. The exterior of the church was stripped of plaster and then faced with flint and dressed stone. The tower has a typical 'Hertfordshire spike' steeple.

39. St Mary's church, c1904. The East Window, seen here, was destroyed during an air raid in the Second World War.

40. St Mary's church in mid-Victorian times, seen from New Street, leading from the market-place. The *One Bell* public house is at the end of the row of houses on the right.

41. The churchyard had many more trees 80 years ago. The earliest part of the church is 13th-century. When the tower was restored, buttresses were added and the builders found evidence of Norman foundations.

42. An Edwardian view of the church. The cottages in the background were demolished many years ago; adjacent to them were the school buildings. The churchyard also contained the vicarage, which was demolished in 1916.

43. A Watford curiosity. The legend of the Fig Tree Tomb was for many years a firm favourite with guide-book writers. The legend was that a Watford man (or woman) died and was a non-believer in the after-life. On his death bed he said that if there was a God, a fig tree would grow out of his heart. This picture shows the tree a century ago, but when the monument later collapsed, it was found that the tree grew from a point nearby and that the incumbent of the tomb had been a devout Christian! The tree was destroyed by the severe weather of 1962-63.

THE FIG TREE, WATFORD.   10
IS FAMOUS ON ACCOUNT OF THE LEGEND OF THE LADY BURIED IN THE VAULT, WHO WAS AN ATHEIST, AND ON HER DEATH-BED
IS REPORTED TO HAVE EXPRESSED A WISH THAT IF THERE WERE A GOD A FIG TREE MIGHT GROW FROM HER HEART.

44. Old churchyards in towns were frequently lined with cottages. This is a view of St Mary's churchyard in 1814. Have the sheep strayed from the nearby market?

45. Church Street with the old school on the left (now demolished) *c.*1908. In the distance can be seen the *One Bell Inn* and New Street. This ancient street just behind the market-place was the site of Ballard's buildings, owned in 1846 by William James Ballard. They became a slum and were pulled down in 1928.

46. Church Street as it is today. The church tower is on the right, and in the distance is the *One Bell* public house.

47.   The Bedford almshouses, built in 1580, are the oldest houses in Watford. They were built by the 2nd Earl of Bedford 'for eight poor women'. The houses were saved from demolition by public subscription in 1931.

48.   The Wesleyan church in Queen's Road by the Broadway and, nearer the camera, the Baptist church. The church with the spire dated from 1889, the architect being Robert Curwen and the cost £17,000. The building was demolished in the 1960s and replaced by a shop and offices. The Baptist church foundation stones were laid by a number of well-known Baptists, including J. P. Barradell, Esq., on 7 September 1887. The church stands at the corner of Grosvenor Road and Derby Road. The original Baptist meeting house was founded in High Street in 1721.

49. St Andrew's church,
Church Road, 1857. The
architect was Sebastian Teulon.

50. St Andrew's church in 1908. The church was erected to serve a new area of the expanding town where many of the railway workers at the L.N.W.R. engineering depot settled.

51. St Michael's and All Angels' church at the junction of Mildred Avenue and Durban Road. The foundation stone was laid on 30 September 1911, and the building consecrated in 1913. Mildred Avenue is named after the benefactor of the church, Mildred Schreiber, who lived at Dalton House in Lower High Street and for many years worked hard raising money to build this church. The streets were laid out at the beginning of the 20th century, hence the names, such as Durban Road. The site was originally the land of Haywood Farm which the Earl of Essex built as a model farm in 1865. Sewerage was pumped from the town to fertilise the meadows!

52. The town cemetery, Vicarage Road, was opened in the 1890s by the Watford Joint Burial Committee, composed of representatives of the Council and local churches.

53. Salters' Company almshouses, Church Road, in 1864. They were designed by Thomas Charles Sorby for the Salters' Company of London. Always confusing to the Watford historian is the fact that there was a second row of Salter's almshouses built by David Salter, a local businessman. They have now been demolished.

54. London Orphan Asylum, which stands north of Junction station. The orphanage, founded in 1813, was originally at Clapham and the Watford settlement was opened in 1871 by Princess Mary, Duchess of Teck. The architect was Henry Dawson.

55. Ancient survival: the Free School of 1704, founded by Dame Elizabeth Fuller of Watford Place 'for the teaching of 40 poor boys and 14 poor girls of Watford in good literature and manners'.

56. Seventh Day Adventist building at Stanborough Park, North Watford, c.1909. Stanborough Park House had belonged
to the Cotterall family. The estate farm specialised in rare breeds of poultry, including Blue Andalusian chickens. The
house (built in 1890) eventually became a fitness club between 1912-63.

57. The Watford Endowed Schools, Derby Road, c.1912. The buildings were opened by the Earl of Clarendon on 20 April
1884.

58.   A fine early view of the old timber-framed Market Hall in 1832. The *One Bell* public house and the church can be seen behind, whilst the town pump with its round wheel (installed in 1819) stands outside the pub. In 1853 fire destroyed the hall and badly damaged adjacent buildings. This view dates from 1832.

59. A sketch showing the market-place as it was in 1830, with the old Market Hall and also the two main hostelries, the *Essex Arms* (left) and the *Rose and Crown* (right). There was a fairly busy coach trade and about fifteen to twenty regular coaches called on weekdays. The ostlers at the *Rose and Crown* wore a uniform of brown jackets and jockey caps, whilst those at the *Essex Arms* wore blue silk jackets and white beaver caps.

60. The market-place 20 years later, not long before the destruction of the Market Hall. The market-place was faced with cobblestones in 1855, by which time the coaching trade had gone and the London and Birmingham Railway sped the long-distance travellers round the northern edge of the town.

61.   Tuesday market about ninety years ago. The *Rose and Crown Hotel* and the old *Compasses Inn* can be seen on the right. Improvements had been made to the former inn and it was advertising 'hacks and hunters of every description for sale'. Despite the railways, some herds of sheep and cattle were still being driven some distance to market. A visitor to Watford market recorded that the drovers seemed to wear their wardrobe of clothes on their backs and carried long sticks. They were accompanied by ragged dogs and poor-looking ponies. Watford had a cattle market on another site until as recently as December 1959.

62.   The market in Edwardian days. In the centre of the picture is the gloomy-looking brick building of the *Rose and Crown Hotel*, which had recently been modernised internally 'with every additional requisite for the comfort of visitors'. Next to it, with the brewer's name 'Sedgewick', is the old *Compasses Inn*. It stood on the site of a much earlier inn and part of an ancient window frame was discovered when the *Compasses* was demolished in 1927-8. It is preserved in the wall of the present commercial buildings at the corner of Market Street, by the post office. The *Rose and Crown* was demolished in 1968 and Boot's was erected on the site. (Boot's has now moved to the Harlequin Centre.)

63. This looks like an early morning picture although the traders have already set up their stalls in the distance. On the right is the *Rose and Crown* where, in the early 19th century, James Rogers, the landlord, was so fat that part of the wall and window frames had to be removed in 1829 when he died. Market Street was created in 1888 by Francis Fisher, who sold his shop on the site and moved to more palatial premises beyond the *Rose and Crown*. He became chairman of Watford Urban District Council 1901-3.

64. The market-place today, looking east. The timbered buildings on the right replaced the old *Compasses* public house in 1928. The modern building on the corner of Market Street (Boot's until recently) replaced the *Rose and Crown Hotel* in 1968-9. The building beyond was once the butcher's shop of Francis Fisher, the developer of Market Street in the 1880s.

65. High Street and the market-place just after the First World War. Just beyond Lloyds Bank (formerly the Bucks and Oxon Bank, rebuilt 1889) is the *Essex Arms Hotel*. It was owned by Trust House Hotels in the 1920s and had a banqueting room to seat 130 guests. Lunch cost 3s. and tea in the lounge 1s. 6d. On the extreme left is Rogers and Gowlet Ltd., 'ironmongers and specialists in lawn mowers ...', established in 1777.

66.   The cattle market in full swing outside the *King's Arms* and Mortimer the butcher's. Mortimer was originally Saunders and Kinders. The other inn shown here is the *Spread Eagle*. The insanitary conditions and the delays to traffic were already a problem by 1914. In 1927 the market franchise was put up for sale by the Earl of Essex, purchased by Mr. Hurst Flint and sold to the council for £19,000. The market was last held in the street in 1929, then moving to another off-street site.

67.   High Street in the tranquil 1900s, with the lime trees that were once a famous landmark by the junction with Clarendon Road. The *Lime Tree Hotel* ('visitors and cyclists welcome – Temperance Hotel') was later replaced by Dudley's, the outfitters, and this spot became known as Dudley's Corner. On the right is the distinctive bay window of Bucks restaurant, where up to 150 people at a time could enjoy lunch for 3s. and tea for 1s. 6d. in the fully licensed restaurant in the 1920s and '30s.

68.   High Street in 1905, with the ivy-clad Upton House and the old fire station. Watford Board of Health moved its offices into Upton House from Local Board Road in 1892. The Board became Watford Urban District Council in 1894 and the house continued to be used as offices until the Town Hall opened in 1938. The buildings seen here were demolished in 1957, their site being used a few years later for Gade House office block and shops.

69.   The *Essex Arms* and adjacent Corn Exchange, which was added in 1858. It was here in 1910 that a programme of 'animated pictures' was shown to an admiring public. The hall and the *Essex Arms* were demolished in 1931 and Cawdell's department store erected in its place.

70. By the early years of the 20th century, the large multiple shops began to appear, although they were nothing like the size we are accustomed to today. Sainsbury's was opened in 1900 at The Parade, High Street.

71. The interior of Watford's first Sainsbury's in 1905. Ladies could sit in one of the chairs whilst pure butter was shaped into half or whole pounds by white-coated assistants, using wooden bats, and the cheese (English or Colonial) cut to requirement with lethal-looking wire. Bacon was sliced to precise thickness by equally dangerous-looking cutting machines. A far cry from the huge Sainsbury's supermarket behind Monmouth House today!

IMPORTERS OF AMERICAN & COLONIAL MEAT

EASTMANS LIMITED

Eastman

72. Hardly hygienic! Eastmans the butcher's at 79 High Street, *c.*1911. It would appear that the meat has been specially displayed for a shopping competition.

73. Another nationwide store that had a branch in Watford in the 1900s was the International Stores. This is their delivery service outside the shop at 98 High Street.

74. High Street, 1921, with the Empress Tea Rooms on the right. The building was erected on the site of Derry House by the Watford Development Company and the Empress restaurant opened on 25 July 1916. There are several stories about whether the building was ever intended as a terminus for the Metropolitan railway. Certainly in 1927 the railway examined the possibility of extending from its terminus at Cassiobury to this site, and land was acquired behind the restaurant 'in anticipation of future requirements'. Later the tea room was sold and became a furnishing store. It is now a branch of Next.

75. The Parade, with Jays Furnishing Store in the 1900s. Albert Clements opened his store here in 1898, and he advertised some time later, 'Our assistants have strict instructions not to press any article on an unwilling customer'. The store, greatly enlarged, is still at the same address.

76.   The Parade and other shops by Clarendon Road were built on the ground which was formerly part of old Watford House (not to be confused with Watford Place). The house was owned by Richard Clutterbuck and there was an ice house in the garden. The remains of this structure were discovered in 1939, but destroyed when air raid shelters were being constructed. In the distance, on the left, are the trees by Upton House, the council offices at that time.

77. James Cawdell and Company's store at 71 High Street, next to the old *Essex Arms Hotel*. Just to the side of Cawdell's is the London City and Midland Bank, the only structure now surviving.

78. A fine early 20th-century photograph of Cawdell's. Cawdell took over George Longley's shop in 1905. The Corn Exchange entrance is on the left. James Cawdell lived over the shop at first, but later he moved to 17 Rickmansworth Road where he died in February 1941.

79. The market-place in the 1930s, with the new Cawdell's on the right. The building incorporated Cawdell's shopping arcade on the site of the *Essex Arms*. At this date, one could have a four-course lunch in the restaurant and listen to a chamber orchestra for about 1s. 10d. (9p).

80. By the 1930s Watford had become a very large and popular shopping centre. This is Cawdell's Easter 1934 advertisement, which offered a dining room suite for just £7.50, although this would have been much more than an average weekly wage in the town at that time.

81. Another view of the 'new' Watford of the inter-war period. A. J. Lyon's delivery van is turning out of Market Street. Beyond Cawdell's is a branch of Timothy White, the chemist. At Cawdell's at this time a high tea with filleted haddock and bread and butter, a pot of tea and a cake, was just the thing for tired shoppers at 1s. (5p).

82. Watford in the late 1940s at the same spot as the previous illustration. London Transport's red 'STL-type' bus on route 142 from West Kilburn, outside the *Rose and Crown*.

83. Moving west along the High Street this view, from the years just after the First World War, shows the shops by the lime trees and Clarendon Road. The Empress Tea Rooms are on the left.

84. High Street looking towards The Parade in the 1930s. There is a London Transport bus in the distance. Bucks restaurant and its bay window is prominent on the left.

85. Philip Buck, 'Cook, caterer for banquets, hunt balls ... catering for the gentry', was a well-known business in High Street until the beginning of the 1960s. This is the original shop with a delivery van at the side.

86. High Street with Bucks café on the left, c.1949. It was still possible to park here whilst doing some shopping.

87. Woolworth's first opened in Watford in 1918. This view shows the store *c*.1937 in the High Street near King Street. Burton's the tailors is next door, and the *King's Arms* is further along. This building was originally the gatehouse to the drive of Watford Place. The whole site here was cleared in the 1960s and the new Woolworth's building was erected. This has recently been demolished and a pair of red-brick buildings constructed, incorporating the MacDonalds fast food shop.

88. King Edward VII in Watford, 7 July 1906. This
illustration comes from a postcard published by Frederick
Downer, a well-known Watford photographer who had
premises at 110 High Street. The 'X' was made on the card
by the sender, who stated: 'Tell your mother Mr. Gibbs the
basketmaker used to live where the 'X' is marked'. It is post
marked 13 October 1907.

89. Mullets hardware shop at 116A High Street dressed for
the 1937 coronation celebrations. Goods in the window
include a kettle for 1s. 6d. and saucepans at 10s. 6d. each.

90. High Street looking towards Queen's Road in 1932. The original premises of Marks and Spencer appear on the right, with the dome of Boot's at the corner of Queen's Road. Marks and Spencer moved to their present site, further along High Street, in 1936.

91. The same view today, with the ancient *One Crown Inn* on the left. This building has a timber frame of the 16th century. The tower with its dome is the new entrance to the Harlequin Centre.

92.   Junction of High Street with King Street and Queen's Road. The building in shadow is Barclays Bank, opened here in 1912. King street is named after Jonathan King, owner of Watford Place from 1826-51. The first mention of what was to be King Street was made in a document of 15 June 1851: 'a street leading out of High Street ... an intended new line of road to Rickmansworth by Colney Butts and the Union'. On the right of the picture, beyond Queen's Road, is the three-storey building of the Westminster Bank.

93.   Another view of the High Street near Queen's Road in 1904. Queen's Road was laid out in the 1860s and that part nearest High Street was at one time called Queen Street. Woolworth's and other shops later occupied the site of the old buildings on the right.

94. South end of High Street, *c*.1905. The row of buildings on the right includes the London Penny Bazaar opened in 1851 where, amongst other things (including an employment agency for domestic servants), Mrs. Goodson sold 'Pure and Wholesome Literature'. The Bazaar and the *George Hotel* were demolished for Marks and Spencer in 1928. 'M and S' later moved slightly nearer to the market-place.

95.　Watford Place is one of the few surviving links with Watford's past. The first house was built in the 16th century by William Heydon. The house seen in this modern view dates from 1790 and was the home of Jonathan King. He sold the lands for building development – hence King Street.

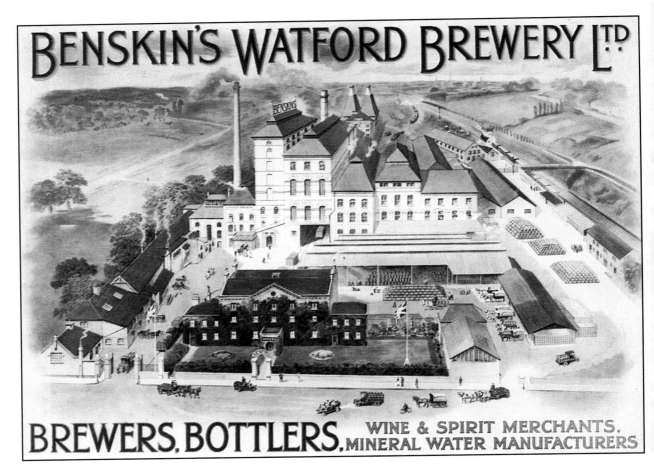

96. Benskin's brewery was for many years the great landmark of Lower High Street. The ivy-covered house in the foreground is now the Watford museum, but everything else has been swept away. Originally the brewery was owned by the Dyson family and the Cannon brewery. Joseph Benskin bought the company in 1867. On the right edge of this old poster can be seen the Watford and Rickmansworth railway, where Benskin's had sidings until 1961. During one period there had been talk of digging a canal branch from the Grand Union Canal. Benskin's were the first company, as far as it is known, to use petrol delivery lorries in Watford, c.1913.

97. The lowest part of the appropriately named Lower High Street was prone to flooding from the Colne for many years. This is a photograph of the floods on 22 July 1907 after a violent thunderstorm. The horse bus is on one of the early local services from Watford Junction and Callowlands to the Bushey Arches.

The Five Arches, Bushey

34305. (JV)

98. The 50-ft. arches of the London and North Western railway crossing the Colne. 'A splendid five-arched construction' according to the *London and Birmingham Railway Guide* of 1840. The foundations were laid on floating brushwood over the very soft ground. Just visible through the arch on the far right is the preserved coal duty boundary marker. The City of London erected these markers around the outskirts of what we now call Greater London, in 1851, and tax ceased in 1889. Watford's first swimming baths were here by the Colne from 1896 to 1933. They had changing huts and a diving board, and were very popular. In 1925, for example, there were 42,150 bathers.

99. No history of Watford is complete without the pond. By the 1900s it had been landscaped, but cattle going to market still used it. In the distance is the crossroads. In the centre grew the Queen's Oak, planted by the Earl of Essex to commemorate the jubilee of 1887. It had to be cut down when the traffic roundabout was laid out in the inter-war years. Now all has changed again and the busy underpass carries non-stop traffic.

100. Holiday scene by High Street pond in 1912. Once Watford had other ponds at Rickmansworth Road, Cassio Hamlet (along Hempstead Road), Clarendon Corner and Little Nascot House. On the left are some of the old houses that were a feature of this part of the High Street. The Shrubberies was the home of the Coles family and Woodlands was the home of the Whirtons.

101. Behind the holiday groups resting on the seat in about 1908 is Darby's Nurseries which ran down to Weymouth Street; there was a footpath just visible to the far right. Beyond the nursery, towards Rickmansworth and St Albans Roads, was the home of John Sedgewick, solicitor and clerk to the Local Board (preceding the Urban District Council). His wife, Emma Oliver, was a landscape painter.

102. This is what the end of High Street by the pond and the busy underpass looked like 90 years ago. The fence on the right is the boundary to Darby's Nursery, and you can just glimpse The Limes through the trees in the middle of the scene.

103. This Edwardian photograph depicts the pond, with a horse and cart taking a wash after the market. A ramp was provided for carts and cattle to enter the fairly shallow water.

104. A stormy day by the High Street pond in 1907.

105. A 1949 view of the pond looking towards The Parade. In the distance on the left is Monmouth House. The original building here was erected in the early 17th century, but was converted into two houses in 1771. In 1816 there were further alterations and additions. in 1927 a major restoration took place, the present front being constructed of bricks salvaged from the then recently demolished Cassiobury House.

106.   Just before the Second World War there were great changes at this end of the High Street. A traffic roundabout was installed, the old houses and their leafy gardens disappeared and parades of smart, but very suburban-looking shops were built. The pond was landscaped and fountains were installed.

107. A final glimpse of the pond and the crossroads – this time it is *c*.1949. Watford Town Hall and its distinctive turret was built on the site of The Elms in 1938/9. The architect was C. Cowles-Voysey and the cost was £186,000. The building contains a fine hall used for concerts and recordings. Until 1936, an A.A. man would control traffic in the rush hour here, giving his salute to all A.A. members as they passed by.

108. The pond as it is today. Shops and offices have replaced the old houses and their walled gardens, and the trees in the distance hide the ugly traffic underpass that has replaced the crossroads.

109. The Peace Memorial hospital was built to commemorate the Watford men who died in the First World War. The building opened on the site of the Essex almshouses in June 1928, the ceremony being conducted by Princess Mary. The hospital closed in May 1985 and is at present derelict.

110. The library was opened on this site in December 1928, replacing the old library in Queen's Road which had been founded in 1874. The semi-detached houses had a short life and were demolished for new roads in the 1970s.

111. High Street by Queen's Road in *c.*1905. The building on the far corner beyond the bank is the Home and Colonial Stores, which was later replaced by Boot's. The corner is now the busy entrance to the Harlequin Centre.

112. The School of Science and Art and the old library in Queen's Road, *c.*1908. The patron was the Earl of Clarendon and the premises were opened in 1874. The site was provided by Thomas Clutterbuck of Watford House. The buildings were gutted by fire in 1966 and Sainsbury's moved to this part of Queen's Road in the early 1970s.

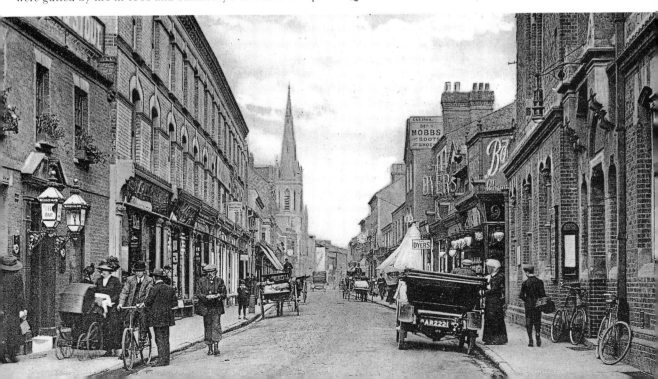

Queen's Road, Watford.

113.   Along the parade of shops in Queen's Road were Trewin's at nos. 20-30 and Coles the photographer at no. 16. In 1906 he announced 'postcard views of the district on sale: sepia platino-types and Cosway prints'. He was still in business after the First World War.

114.   A family portrait. Mr. and Mrs. F. T. Trewin are in the garden of their home, at 12 Upton Road, in 1906. Mr. Trewin's brother, Arthur, took over an existing draper's shop at 28 Queen's Road in 1880, and was later joined by other members of the family. Trewin Brothers (later part of the John Lewis Partnership) remained in Queen's Road until 1990, when the new store opened in the Harlequin Centre.

115.   Watford has been fortunate in having three department stores for many years. An advertisement of 1926 stated: 'Trewins has become more than ever the shopping centre where everything for the home and the wardrobe can be obtained – at Watford's lowest prices – always'. The store had just opened a John Quality food department in the basement.

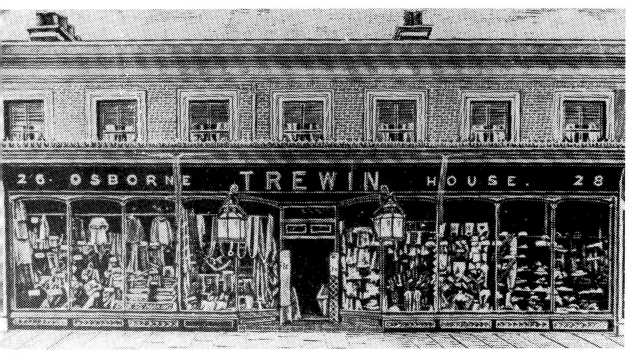

116. Edwardian summer in Queen's Road, with J. B. Field, the draper, on the left. Today this part of the street has completely disappeared, covered by the Harlequin development.

117. Queen's Road as it is today. The new Harlequin Centre has almost eclipsed what was Queen's Road. The right-hand side of the Centre stands on the site of the old Art School and the original library.

118. Queen's Road today. The imposing entrance to the new centre echoes the architecture of the original buildings here, which housed Watford's first Boot's. Only the bank on the left remains of the original Queen's Road-High Street corner.

119. The Watford Co-operative store as it was in Queen's Road in the 1920s. The Co-op moved to Gade House, where its new large store was opened by the mayor in 1965.

120. This photograph of 1909 shows Elliott's music shop, which was in The Broadway, Queen's Road. The store later moved to 16 High Street.

PALACE THEATRE,

WATFORD,

WILL OPEN

MONDAY, DECEMBER 14th,
1908,

With a High-Class

Vaudeville Company,

UNDER THE DIRECTION OF T. M. SYLVESTER.

The Booking Office at the Palace will be open on Saturday, December 12th, from 10 a.m. until 4 p.m., for those who are desirous of having their seats reserved for the Opening Night.

The Hall will be open for Inspection on the same day. Any person wishing to inspect the Building must first apply to the Management for a pass entitling them to view the Palace Theatre.

SEE FURTHER ANNOUNCEMENTS.

121.   As Watford grew, so there was a demand for entertainment. No go-ahead town could be without a theatre, and the Palace opened in 1908. Drama had originally been presented a century or more before at the *Wheatsheaf Inn*, at the very bottom of Lower High Street near the river. The Palace was built on what had been the tea gardens of The Limes in Clarendon Road/High Street. Originally it had been intended to call the theatre the New Theatre, and it appears that the name change was made only at the last minute. The exterior of the building was improved within a few years. The theatre attracted many great names of pre-1914 Music Hall, and in more recent times, the Palace saw the premier of Pinter's *The Homecoming*. Next door there was a skating rink for many years until it later became the Carlton cinema (now demolished).

122. The Watford Electric Coliseum, St Alban's Road, *c*.1919. There were seats to suit all – with prices from 3d. to the
very best at 1s. This cinema opened in 1918.

123. The Central Hall Picture House, King Street, which advertised in the 1920s: 'always a reliable programme, accompanied by a first class orchestra'. Here one could forget the dull, wet streets outside and relax in the 6d., 1s. or 2s. 4d. seats.

124. The Essoldo, King Street, converted from the old Central Hall Cinema in 1928. By the time this photograph was taken about twenty years ago, the films had been replaced by the excitements of Bingo.

125. The Empire Picture Hall, 'Where the Best Pictures are', opened before the First World War, and is now the sole survivor of numerous cinemas that could once be found in Watford.

126.   The Gartlet school in Clarendon Road was one of many private educational establishments in Watford. In 1939 the principals were Miss Sell and Miss May. The school had a large gymnasium and tennis facilities and pupils were 'escorted to the bus and trains'. Gartlet Road is a reminder of the school. In 1906 Shirley House school was 'For gentlemen's sons between the age of 7 and 14 to prepare for the Public Schools and the Navy'. This school was in Langley Road, but moved to Red Heath in 1918.

127.   It hardly seems possible that the horseman is at the junction of St Albans Road and Station Road. The picture is taken from Langley Road looking towards the Junction. Most of the houses have now gone – either for road widening or office blocks.

128. St Albans Road developed from mid-Victorian times, and by 1900 had become a mixture of private houses, shops and even hotels. For example, in 1925 the *Woolger Hotel* at no. 129 had all the modern amenities of electric light and a bathroom with hot and cold water, and was situated just two minutes walk from the station.

129. In this modern photograph, it can be seen that Station Road has been widened and the huge bulk of the station office block dominates the end of the street.

130.   The St Albans Road area was developed as Watford New Town from c.1887. The Watford Electric Coliseum opened in 1918 with a programme of moving pictures accompanied by a pianist. Later came the Odeon of 1938 (not to be confused with the later Odeon in central Watford).

131.   Shops for all classes. Jarvis Stores in St Albans Road offered all kinds of discounted goods, for this picture was taken in the days of the Depression.

132.   Hempstead Road looking towards the crossroads and the town. Cassio Hamlet was a collection of cottages that were swept away when Hempstead Road was widened and modern houses built in the 1920s. The College of Further Education now stands on the right.

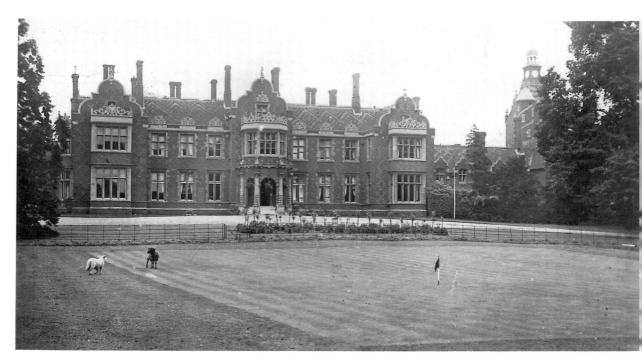

133. Just the other side of Bushey Arches is Bushey Hall. It was built in 1865 for Edward Marjoribanks, but became a health hydro in 1896. By 1926 it was advertising in the guide-books as an hotel: 'an ideal spot for colonials and visitors from the east ... 35 minutes from Baker Street on the Bakerloo Tube'.

134. The narrow bridge under the St Albans branch line at Balmoral Road in 1948. The advertisements include the Carlton cinema ('No Orchids for Miss Blandish') and John Black presenting music at the Town Hall. Balmoral Road, Sandringham Road and others were named after the royal estates. Industry developed here after 1900 and included Dr. Tibb's Vi-Cocoa ('the food beverage of the people') works at Delectaland. The works were badly damaged by a fire in 1903.

135. Russell Farm Lodge was an outpost of the vast Cassiobury lands and is shown in this sketch of 1837. The lodge stood by Beechwood Rise in St Albans Road.

136. Transport was vital to the development of Watford in the 19th century, but roads remained very poor until almost the end of that century. This stylised view of Aldenham Road shows a typical rural highway a century ago.

137. The coming of the Grand Junction canal at the end of the 18th century did not really affect Watford, because its route passed well to the south and west. This sketch shows the canal about 125 years ago, looking towards Cassiobury bridge and locks.

138. Powered canal boat and 'butty' (towed craft) in the locks at Cassiobury, 1908.

139. The canal above the lock, with Cassiobury Park on the right. On the left a horse is pulling the long rope attached to the canal craft in the distance. A slow but peaceful means of transport in 1908.

140. Watford tunnel soon after completion in 1837. The tunnel under part of the Cassiobury estate was totally unnecessary, but the Earl of Essex did not want the railway either seen or heard from his estate. As a result, 11 men died while digging the tunnel through treacherous chalk and many more were injured.

141. Traffic so increased after the London and Birmingham railway became the London and North Western in 1856 that a second tunnel had to be made in 1875.

142.   The first Watford station was sited north of the St Albans Road bridge and one building still survives. This is the newer Junction station in 1860 (the St Albans branch opened in 1858). To cater for a new class of business traveller and family, the *Clarendon Hotel* was opened at the same time.

143. The *Clarendon Hotel* in 1860. It has recently been called one of the outstanding architectural hotels and inns in modern Hertfordshire. Only part of it is now in use as a bar.

144. An early 20th-century photograph of the *Clarendon Hotel* and Junction station, with an L.N.W.R. 'feeder' bus. Amongst the amenities of electric light and hot water there were also tennis courts at the hotel.

145. Watford was growing rapidly and a better train service to London was needed. The so-called 'New Lines' were added in 1912 from London to Watford, but with a completely new line from Bushey round by Watford Fields to join the old Rickmansworth branch at High Street, the line here being doubled to the Junction. This picture shows a 'New Line' rush hour train taking City workers from Watford to Broad Street on 18 February 1912.

146. Northbound to Birmingham in Edwardian days at Bushey troughs. Locomotives could pick up water here at speed – the first place on the down journey from Euston. The locomotive is *King Arthur*.

147. Watford locomotive shed was not very large, but it did house locomotives such as this one, seen with a branch line train at Watford Junction on 18 June 1932, probably bound for St Albans.

148. 'Live in the country' – a poster issued for the New Lines from 1912. Electrification was slow in being put into operation and the L.N.W.R. electric trains did not start until after the First World War. This poster was issued for the New Lines on 10th February 1913.

LIVE IN THE COUNTRY.

The Opening of the New L. & N.W. Line between Willesden and Watford on February 10th with new stations at Harlesden, Stonebridge Park, North Wembley, Kenton, Headstone Lane, Watford West, and Croxley Green, has opened up an entirely new Residential District to the City Man.

This District has been very appropriately called

LONDON'S BEAUTIFUL NORTH-WEST

and, commencing February 10th, the train service from and to Euston will be considerably augmented, making it especially convenient to the City Man.

Cheap Rents.   Perfect Sanitation.   Good Schools.
Excellent Golf Courses.   Ample Water Supply.

Send a post card to Enquiry Office, Euston Station, N.W., for free booklet entitled "North-Western Country Homes."

North-Western Country Homes.

149. At the Junction on a quiet Sunday morning in the late 1930s. There is a poster advertising a cheap trip to Dublin for only 21s. 6d. Note the London Underground sign next to the poster. The café lasted until the late 1970s and the station has now been completely rebuilt.

150. Bakerloo tube train composed of ex-Central London line stock, c.1917, soon after services began. L.N.W.R. electric trains did not begin until 1922. This was the furthest tube trains travelled at this time. In the 1920s more comfortable trains were specially built for the Watford 'joint' service; they were even fitted with luggage racks.

151. A rare photograph of a tube-stock train in 1917 heading from High Street to the newly-built Croxley electric depot. The Bakerloo service to Watford began on 16 April 1917.

152. In 1922 the L.N.W.R./L.M.S. commenced the electric services from Euston, and Broad Street to Watford, Croxley, Rickmansworth and to Earl's Court and Richmond. The trains were known as the 'Oerlikon stock' after the Swiss manufacturers of their electric gear. They were some of the most luxurious suburban trains around London. The last train of this type was withdrawn in 1960, but one car has been preserved.

153. Watford main line south of Watford and *Princess Mary Rose* with the *Mid-day Scot* express for Glasgow.

"METRO" AND L.N.E.R.

WATFORD'S NEW RAILWAY

PARTICULARS OF TRAIN SERVICE AND SEASON TICKET RATES LONDON AND CROXLEY GREEN AND WATFORD.

2nd NOVEMBER, 1925.

Knapp, Drewett & Sons Ltd., Kingston-on-Thames and London.—11424 W.

154. Plans for a Metropolitan branch line to Watford were first announced in 1912, but it was not until 1925 that they became a reality. This booklet was issued a few weeks before the line opened and booking offices for the sale of season tickets were at Croxley and Watford.

155. Logan and Hemingway had a formidable task constructing the Metropolitan railway. Pile drivers are hard at work making the foundations for the bridge over the Gade and the canal near Cassio bridge in the winter of 1923. Much of the earth for the very high embankment here came from the deep cuttings south of Croxley station.

156. The official opening train on 31 October 1925 at Croxley, bound for Watford. There were 20 electric locomotives of this type, later mainly used on Rickmansworth to London trains. Number 12, seen here, was later named *Sarah Siddons*, after the famous 18th-century actress, and is still in existence, being occasionally used for special railway tours.

157. Gala day at the new Metropolitan station on 31 October 1925. The guests later travelled by coach and car to a special lunch at the Oddfellows' Hall in St Albans Road.

158. The opening of the Metropolitan at Watford. Lord Faringdon on the left represented the L.N.E.R. which was jointly responsible for the services; Lord Aberconway, chairman of the Metropolitan railway, is on the right; in the centre is Alderman M. A. Thorpe, Mayor of Watford.

159. The official opening at Watford, with guests inspecting the spacious new station. Goods yards covered several acres, and included a warehouse and facilities for handling all kinds of goods, including cattle.

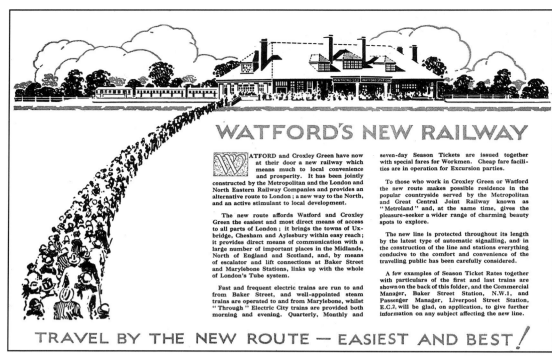

WATFORD'S NEW RAILWAY

WATFORD and Croxley Green have now at their door a new railway which means much to local convenience and prosperity. It has been jointly constructed by the Metropolitan and the London and North Eastern Railway Companies and provides an alternative route to London; a new way to the North, and an active stimulant to local development.

The new route affords Watford and Croxley Green the easiest and most direct means of access to all parts of London; it brings the towns of Uxbridge, Chesham and Aylesbury within easy reach; it provides direct means of communication with a large number of important places in the Midlands, North of England and Scotland, and, by means of escalator and lift connections at Baker Street and Marylebone Stations, links up with the whole of London's Tube system.

Fast and frequent electric trains are run to and from Baker Street, and well-appointed steam trains are operated to and from Marylebone, whilst "Through" Electric City trains are provided both morning and evening. Quarterly, Monthly and

seven-day Season Tickets are issued together with special fares for Workmen. Cheap fare facilities are in operation for Excursion parties.

To those who work in Croxley Green or Watford the new route makes possible residence in the popular countryside served by the Metropolitan and Great Central Joint Railway known as "Metroland" and, at the same time, gives the pleasure-seeker a wider range of charming beauty spots to explore.

The new line is protected throughout its length by the latest type of automatic signalling, and in the construction of the line and stations everything conducive to the comfort and convenience of the travelling public has been carefully considered.

A few examples of Season Ticket Rates together with particulars of the first and last trains are shown on the back of this folder, and the Commercial Manager, Baker Street Station, N.W.1, and Passenger Manager, Liverpool Street Station, E.C.2, will be glad, on application, to give further information on any subject affecting the new line.

TRAVEL BY THE NEW ROUTE — EASIEST AND BEST!

160.   Unfulfilled dreams. No crowds (unless Watford F.C. is playing at home) have ever used Watford Metropolitan station, but there were high hopes in 1925.

161.   A 1925 poster advertising the new station.

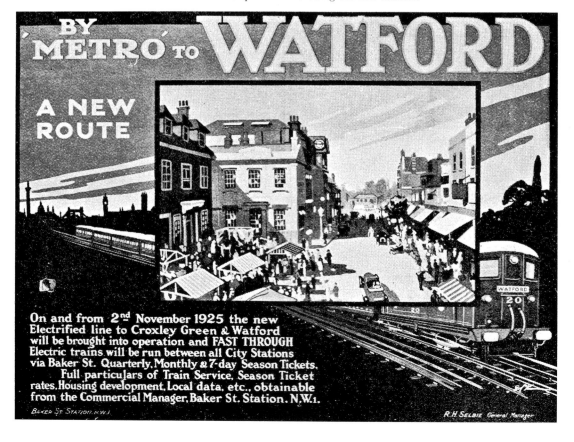

162. The former Empress tearooms and restaurant in High Street was offered for sale in 1928. Metropolitan posters were displayed at the premises for some years, but the dream of extending the line from Cassiobury Park was never realised.

To **REACH** ANY **PART** OF **LONDON** **QUICKLY** . **AND** IN **COMFORT,** **TRAVEL FROM CROXLEY GREEN** OR **WATFORD** STATIONS (LONDON TRANSPORT & L·N·E·R)

Through Electric Trains run to and from the City throughout the day. At Baker Street and Marylebone the train services connect with the **UNDERGROUND** for West End.

Cheap Day Tickets at about the single fare for the return journey are issued to Baker Street and Marylebone and all London and Suburban stations on the Metropolitan Line, Weekdays after 10 a.m., Sundays by all trains. Cheap Day Tickets are issued similarly to stations between Harrow and Verney Junction on Wednesdays and Saturdays after 10 a.m., Sundays by all trains (except stations closed on Sundays).

Quarterly, Monthly and Seven-day Season Tickets and Workmen's Tickets are available.

A frequent Service of Buses runs between Watford Station and the High Street, Watford.

163. This Metropolitan poster (preserved in an album – hence the distortion!) is dated c.1927. Note the bottom line advertising the special bus services into the town centre.

164. The Watford terminus was designed by the railway's own architect Charles W. Clarke in a suburban villa style to blend with the surrounding houses. It is interesting that the newsagents and sweetshop on the left is still there in 1992.

165. From 1927–33 sets of electric compartment-stock trains were introduced for the Watford services. Later known as the 'T' stock they lasted until 1962. Note the cattle dock on the far right. The station sign is of the typical Metropolitan red diamond type with blue and white cross bar. The signs remained here until the mid-1950s.

166. A Metropolitan feeder bus – one of the 28-seater Albion vehicles that commenced running a service that connected with every train. The buses cost £396 and were later operated by the Lewis bus company.

WATFORD STATION

WATFORD SHOPPING WEEK

METROPOLITAN RAILWAY

METROPOLITAN RAILWAY.

167.   Dressed for the day – the Metropolitan buses won a prize in the Watford Shopping Week in October 1928. The bus on the left (Number 4) was sold in 1934 and the other bus (Number 2) in April 1936 to G. J. Dawson for scrapping. The buses were kept in a smart garage opposite the station forecourt. There were also facilities for servicing the cars of more wealthy passengers. The garage (by then for cars only) closed in 1963 and houses were built on the site.

168. An early L.N.W.R. bus service for Watford to Harrow (Wealdstone) using Milnes-Daimler buses began on 23 April 1906. The single fare to Harrow was 4d. Later routes were Watford Junction to Croxley Green (1913) and by 1914 there were 20 L.N.W.R. buses in the Watford area and a London General red bus from South Harrow (route 173 Sundays only). All railway buses ceased in Watford in 1915 and were not resumed by the L.N.W.R. after the war.

169. A fine array of open coaches of the Lewis Omnibus Co. in the market-place in the 1920s. Lewis's office was at 25 Market Street.

170.   London General bus in Watford in 1932. The main bus company (after the Lewis company) was the National Bus Co. formed in February by Thomas Clarkson. By 1933 routes were operating all over Hertfordshire, and into Bedfordshire and Essex. The London General Country Bus Company was formed by the long-established London General on 1 March 1932. All the local companies were gradually absorbed into the new London Passenger Transport Board after July 1933.

171. The Lewis Omnibus Company dates back to 1920 and by the end of that decade operated buses from Watford to St Albans, Rickmansworth, the Chilterns and even Windsor. It became a subsidiary of the North West Land and Transport Company (part of the Metropolitan railway) in 1926 but operated as the Lewis Omnibus Co. This bus was photographed in July 1930.

172. Preserved early Green Line coach. The first Green Line route to Watford began operation on 2 October 1929 from Golders Green. There was also a fast express coach service (the Bucks Express) operated from High Street by Bucks Café with 'luxurious and comfortable coaches' to Oxford Circus from 29 September 1929. From 18 December 1929 the Green Line route W began from Watford to Charing Cross. Route J dates from October 1933.

173.   Finally, for something different in local transport: shunting at Croxley paper mills in 1940. Paper-making began in Watford in the 18th century. The mills at Watford west date from 1830 but were greatly extended in 1886. For many years the distinctive smell of esparto grass (used in the manufacturing process) was familiar to the inhabitants of this part of the town. Rail operations (with diesels) ceased on 20 November 1983.

174.   Industry and design: the Odhams building was designed by Sir Owen Williams in 1937 and stood near the new Watford bypass. This great temple of printing employed 2,700 people when this picture was taken in the early 1960s, and produced more than seven million copies of magazines weekly. The plant closed in 1983 and is now a supermarket.

175. Watford at war. Firemen outside the badly damaged Trewin's Store in Queen's Road after an air raid in January 1941.

176. First World War Peace Parade, Cassiobury Park, 1919. Watford Council purchased part of the ancient parklands as a public open space in 1912, adding further large areas in the 1920s.

177. A farewell to Watford. Cassiobury lock and the lock keeper's house in 1905, long before traffic thundered along the nearby roads, at a time when Watford town centre still resembled a market town.